W9-CFV-541

FREEDOM FORCES

★U.S. COAST GUARD★

HIGH SEAS ADVENTURE

Piper Welsh

Rourke
Educational Media
rourkeeducationalmedia.com

Scan for Related Titles and
Teacher Resources

www.rourkeeducationalmedia.com

PHOTO CREDITS: Cover: Official USCG photo by PA1 Kurt Fredrickson, radar screen background on cover and pages © SkillUp; flag on back cover and title page © SFerdon; Page 4 © Rembrandt Peale 1854; Page 5 © John Trumbull 1804, James A. Mitchell, III, ildogesto; Page 6 © Illustrated London News; Page 7 © US Coast guard, ildogesto; Page 9 © ildogesto; Page 10 © National Archives & Records Administration; Page 11 © ildogesto; Page 13 © Tom Sperduto; Page 14/15 © Petty Officer 1st Class Michael O'Day US Navy; Page 16 © U.S. Coast Guard, John Edwards; Page 17 © U.S. Coast Guard; Page 18 © Petty Officer 2nd Class Lauren Jorgensen; Page 19 © U.S. Coast Guard, U.S. Navy; Page 20 © Isaac Pacheco, Petty Officer 2nd Class Charly Hengen; Page 21 © Petty Officer 3rd Class Cynthia Oldham, U.S. Coast Guard; Pages 22 and 23 © U.S. Coast Guard; Page 24 © Mass Communications Specialist 1st Class Corey Lewis US Navy; Page 25 © U.S. Coast Guard, Petty Officer 1st Class Michael Anderson U.S. Coast Guard; Page 26 © Mass Communication Specialist 2nd Class Stuart Phillips, Petty Officer 3rd Class Jon-Paul; Rios, PA1 Timothy Tamargo; Page 27 © Petty Officer 1st Class Luke Pinneo; Pages 28 and 29 © NOAA;

Edited by Precious McKenzie

Designed and Produced by Blue Door Publishing, FL

Library of Congress Cataloging-in-Publication Data

U.S. Coast Guard: High Seas Adventure / Piper Welsh
  p. cm. -- (Freedom Forces)
  ISBN 978-1-62169-924-8 (hard cover) (alk. paper)
  ISBN 978-1-62169-819-7 (soft cover)
  ISBN 978-1-62717-028-4 (e-book)
Library of Congress Control Number: 2013938876

Also Available as:
ROURKE'S
e-Books

Rourke Educational Media
Printed in the United States of America,
North Mankato, Minnesota

Rourke
Educational Media

rourkeeducationalmedia.com
customerservice@rourkeeducationalmedia.com
PO Box 643328 Vero Beach, Florida 32964

TABLE OF CONTENTS

CHAPTER ONE

THANK YOU, GEORGE WASHINGTON!

After the United States won its independence from Great Britain, **smugglers** continued to run the coastlines, not paying taxes on the goods they were carrying and selling. The young United States was losing millions of desperately needed dollars. But, Alexander Hamilton had a plan to stop smugglers and send the lost dollars right into the U.S. Treasury. In April of 1790, Hamilton asked Congress to build maritime vessels to combat smuggling and regain lost tax dollars. By August of 1790, George Washington signed the Tariff Act. With Washington's signature on this historic act, ten vessels were built to enforce the nation's tariffs and collect revenue.

George Washington
1732-1799

Coast Guard Cutters
The first ten vessels were called cutters, and the early Coast Guard was called the Revenue Cutter Service. It was renamed the Coast Guard in 1915.

After the American Revolution, the United States was $75 million in debt. Alexander Hamilton, the first Secretary of the Treasury, wanted to pay off the debt as quickly as possible. He believed "The debt of the United States … was the price of liberty."

Alexander Hamilton
1755-1804

The Coast Guard did not stay close to American coasts. Their duty was to patrol and protect the high seas from smugglers and pirates. Vessels traveled to remote and dangerous places such as Paraguay, Mexico, and the far reaches of Alaska. Coast Guard cutters represented the law in lawless lands and the open seas.

U.S. Revenue Cutter *Bear*, circa 1890 on Patrol off Alaska.

CHAPTER TWO THE DARING BERING SEA PATROL

After the United States purchased Alaska in 1867, Coast Guard cutters had to tackle the treacherous conditions of the icy Bering Strait. Why did the United States need a patrol in the frigid Arctic Zone? One of their main duties was monitoring and enforcing the hunting of fur seals.

The Bering Sea Patrol had other important duties in remote northern waters. When whalers and steam ships got stuck on ice or stranded at sea, it was the Bering Sea Patrol to the rescue. The Bering Sea Patrol operated many life-saving expeditions. They even carried food and medical supplies to remote Alaskan villages. The ship's doctor would help sick or injured natives in Alaska or Siberia.

Great Britain and the United States almost went to war over seals in th 1890s. The seal pelts were a huge source of revenue for companies around the world. However, the United States wanted to protect the seals' breeding grounds from hunting. The Revenue Cutter Service policed the frigid waters off Alas to make sure no one was hunting the seals illegally.

The infamous Overland Relief Expedition during the winter of 1897, required the Coast Guard's bravery and skills. Eight whaling ships were trapped in thick ice fields around Point Barrow. Without a way to get free from the ice, the whalers would starve to death. On December 16, 1897, the rescuers began their dangerous voyage using skis, snowshoes, and dog sleds pulled by reindeer. They fought sub zero temperatures, blinding blizzards, and thick Arctic darkness. Then, on March 29, 1898, the rescuers made it to Point Barrow. The expedition brought food to the starved and stranded whalers, in the form of 382 reindeer!

Point Barrow

Bering Strait

Alaska

Arctic Ocean

HERO HIGHLIGHT

Captain Ellsworth Price Bertholf was the first commandant of the Coast Guard. Congress awarded him the Gold Medal of Honor for his part in the Point Barrow-Overland Relief Expedition.

Captain Ellsworth Price Bertholf

1866-1921

CHAPTER THREE

ALWAYS READY

The Coast Guard is always ready to fight and defend. Since its creation in 1790, the Coast Guard has faced action in every conflict fought by the United States. As part of the Department of the Navy in World War I, the Coast Guard lost more lives in **convoy** and patrol than any other military branch.

During World War II, the Coast Guard took a central role in defeating the Nazis. Brave Coast Guard crews battled Hitler's submarines and U-boats in treacherous waters. They fought tirelessly and managed to sink 13 of Hitler's U-boats, protecting Europe from total Nazi domination.

During WWII, German submarines were called U-boats, a short version of *Unterseeboot*, German for undersea boat. German U-boats were designed to destroy enemy ships and to kill the allies.

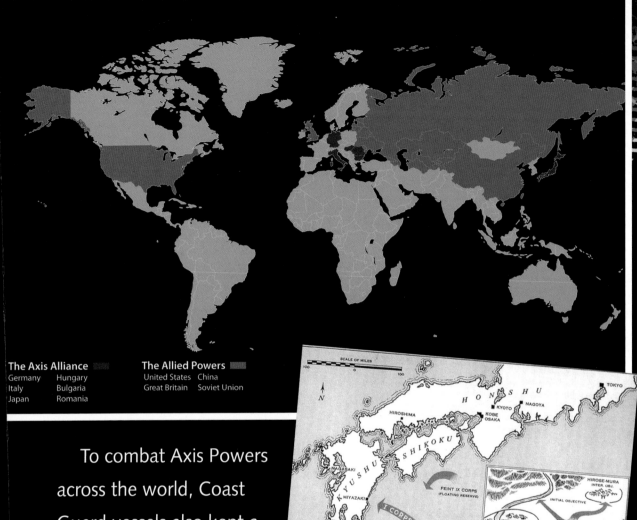

The Axis Alliance
Germany   Hungary
Italy   Bulgaria
Japan   Romania

The Allied Powers
United States   China
Great Britain   Soviet Union

OPERATION OLYMPIC
THE PLANNED INVASION OF JAPAN BY
THE SIXTH ARMY 1 NOV 45

To combat Axis Powers across the world, Coast Guard vessels also kept a close and critical watch over the Pacific. In their mission to protect and preserve democracy during World War II, the Coast Guard destroyed two enemy Japanese submarines. They also made top secret plans, which they called Operation Olympic, to invade Japan. Japan surrendered in August 1945, before the Coast Guard could invade the island.

Operation Olympic was the code name for a planned landing in Kyushu. The invasion was planned for November 1, 1945, with three landings at three different beaches.

Bold Coast Guard crew members served in many bloody missions during World War II. They faced death as they fought against Nazi forces in Europe. In France alone, the Coast Guard was instrumental. During Operation Overlord, on D-Day, Coast Guard forces rescued over 1,500 torpedoed survivors.

The hand painted skull and crossbones on the USCG-6 off Normandy represents a unit identification insignia or victory flag.

USCG 6

Think Africa did not play a role in World War II? Think again. Germany was trying to gain a stronghold in Africa. But the Coast Guard was ready to fight. They led Operation Torch, as part of the **offensive** against Germany. For the first time in history, American and British troops worked together to plan an invasion. Troops landed at Casablanca, Algiers, and Oran. And, one by one, the Allied Forces conquered them all.

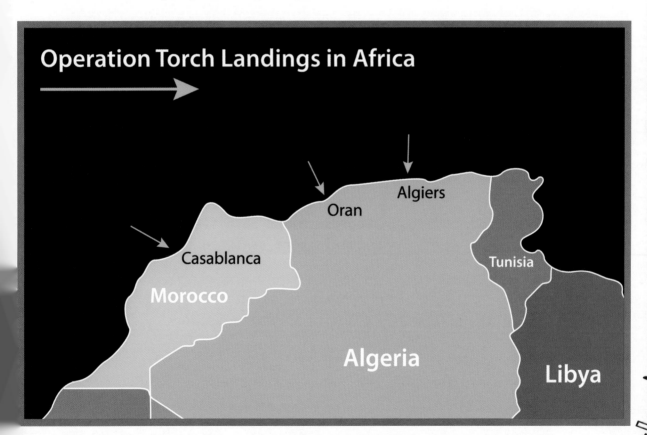

Operation Torch Landings in Africa

The Allies organized three amphibious task forces to seize the key ports and airports of Morocco and Algeria simultaneously, targeting Casablanca, Oran, and Algiers. Successful completion of these operations was to be followed by an eastward advance into Tunisia.

When tensions began to rise in Vietnam during the 1960s, the Coast Guard was ready. The Navy teamed up with the Coast Guard because they desperately needed shallow water vessels in order to get inshore. Coast Guard vessels patrolled inland waterways and guarded the coastline. They also performed the dangerous work of intercepting vessels, searching for **contraband**, and supplying fire support for their allies. Part of their most important work in Southeast Asia was their key role in the set up and operation of Loran C, a long range navigational system. The Loran C assisted the U.S. Air Force warplanes with precision navigation during their air strikes and reconnaissance.

The Coast Guard played a significant role in securing Vietnam's 1,200-mile (1931.21 kilometer) coastline. Some 8,000 Coast Guardsmen and 56 different combatant vessels were assigned to duty there.

COAST GUARD

The Coast Guard is ever vigilant and prepared for any situation. In more recent years, the Coast Guard worked to liberate Panama in 1989. In 1990, the Coast Guard worked directly with the United Nations to police sanctions in the Middle East. On September 11, 2001, when the World Trade Center was attacked, Coast Guard crews mobilized immediately. They were some of the first responders to help those in need and provide security to the area.

The U.S. Coast Guard coordinated the evacuation of half a million people from lower Manhattan after 9/11. Tugs, ferries, police launches, fireboats, and other watercraft converged on lower Manhattan as Coast Guard personnel and vessels directed boat traffic through the smoke and carried out the largest maritime evacuation in world history.

CHAPTER FOUR THE LAW OF THE SEA

The Coast Guard has a fierce combination of military and law enforcement duties. That is what makes the U.S. Coast Guard unlike any other branch of the armed services. As part of their mission, they intercept terrorists, drug smugglers, and pirates.

The USCG is in charge of the U.S. Maritime Defense Zone. They must be vigilant as they protect U.S. coasts, ports, and waterways.

Coast Guard patrols navigate South American waters, watching for signs of illegal drug smugglers. Often, the drug smugglers have high caliber machine guns and are ready to fight. The Coast Guard doesn't back down. Their job is to stop the illegal drugs from reaching American streets.

Each year thousands of **migrants** try to sneak into the United States illegally. Migrants try to smuggle themselves into the United States on overloaded boats, posing imminent danger to themselves and others. Some migrants are part of illicit human **trafficking** rings, those trying to send women or children to other countries as slaves. The Coast Guard is always prepared to intercept them, protect the innocent, and enforce the law.

The Coast Guard's duty is to prevent the loss of life at sea. They completely support the path to legal U.S. immigration.

Because of intricate international laws, the Coast Guard must navigate a complex system that includes **foreign** countries, other branches of the military, and the Department of Homeland Security, as they work toward justice.

BIOMETRICS

Thanks to new technology, the Coast Guard uses biometrics when dealing with migrants. A biometric profile records biographic data, fingerprints, and a facial portrait. The Coast Guard sends the biometric file to the Department of Homeland Security. After Homeland Security processes the file, the results are sent back to the Coast Guard. Then the Coast Guard can take the proper law enforcement action.

The USCG works with other federal agencies and foreign countries in the interception of illegal migrants at sea. The migrants are then denied entry into the United States.

CHAPTER FIVE

SEARCH AND RESCUE

The Coast Guard is a well-trained team of rapid responders in crisis situations. When there's a distress call, the Coast Guard mobilizes. Their crews perform treacherous sea rescues using ships, helicopters, planes, and parachutes. No mission is impossible.

A crew member aboard Coast Guard Cutter *Morro Bay* pulls a fellow Coast Guardsman out of the water while practicing ice rescue techniques.

HERO HIGHLIGHT

When the fishing vessel *Megan Marie* called for help as it was taking on water, Pearson and his team manually prevented the fishing vessel's engine from shutting down so that the rescue mission could be completed safely for all involved.

MK2 *Josh Pearson*
MACHINERY TECHNICIAN

The U.S. Coast Guard demonstrates how they conduct a search and rescue during the 2009 Sea and Sky Spectacular.

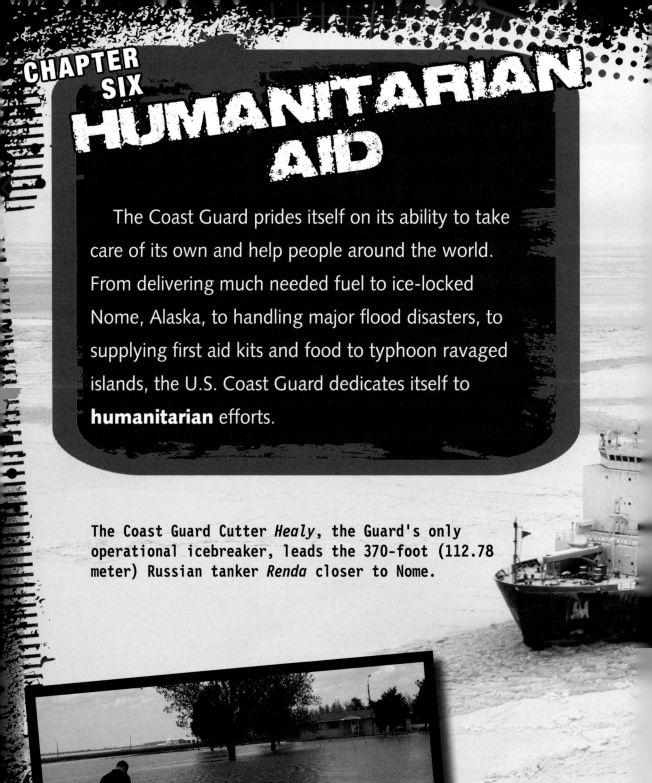

CHAPTER SIX
HUMANITARIAN AID

The Coast Guard prides itself on its ability to take care of its own and help people around the world. From delivering much needed fuel to ice-locked Nome, Alaska, to handling major flood disasters, to supplying first aid kits and food to typhoon ravaged islands, the U.S. Coast Guard dedicates itself to **humanitarian** efforts.

The Coast Guard Cutter *Healy*, the Guard's only operational icebreaker, leads the 370-foot (112.78 meter) Russian tanker *Renda* closer to Nome.

A Coast Guard Reservist wades out into a water-covered driveway that his disaster area response team had crossed to rescue a couple trapped in their home by floodwater.

A Coast Guard MH-65 Dolphin helicopter from Air Station Atlantic City, N.J., patrols above Long Island Sound, which was heavily impacted by Hurricane Sandy, November 6, 2012. The upgraded MH-65Ds from Atlantic City were instrumental in responding to the storm.

U.S. COAST GUARD

Coast Guard Cutter Sequoia anchored off the island of Nomwin while the local children gathered around the shore waiting for the small boat to transfer supplies.

CHAPTER SEVEN
GUARDIANS OF THE ENVIRONMENT

Across vast oceans, the U.S. Coast Guard is committed to protecting the sea and its creatures. They keep a vigilant watch in the fight against **pollution**. They combat violators of international fishing laws. They rescue stranded or injured marine animals. And, they are strategically looking for ways to go green and become more fuel efficient.

A four-acre field of solar arrays will provide the Coast Guard Training Center (TRACEN) Petaluma's with its daily power needs.

An Alaska SeaLife Center employee prepares a walrus calf for transport aboard a Coast Guard Air Station Kodiak HC-130 Hercules airplane in Barrow, Alaska.

THE LATEST TECHNOLOGY

The Coast Guard stays on top of the latest technology so they can remain the dominant force at sea. Computer technology plays a large part in keeping America safe. Terrorists have positioned themselves to perform **cyber attacks** on the world. The Coast Guard monitors and intercepts potential cyber attacks by using highly skilled intelligence officers at U.S. Cyber Command.

Coast Guard engineers tirelessly design and maintain the **fleet**. In order to remain the best at sea, their ships must be able to perform. The engineers are always testing new designs to keep America ahead of the enemy.

Sailors on the watch floor of the Navy Cyber Defense Operations Command monitor, analyze, detect, and defensively respond to unauthorized activity within U.S. Navy information systems and computer networks.

A Coast Guard 32-foot (9.75 meter) Transportable Port Security Boat arrives at Naval Station Guantanamo Bay. Port Security used the boat to secure the port and waterways around the naval station.

he EADS HC-144 Ocean Sentry is a medium-range, twin-engine ircraft used by the U.S. Coast Guard in search and rescue nd maritime patrol missions.

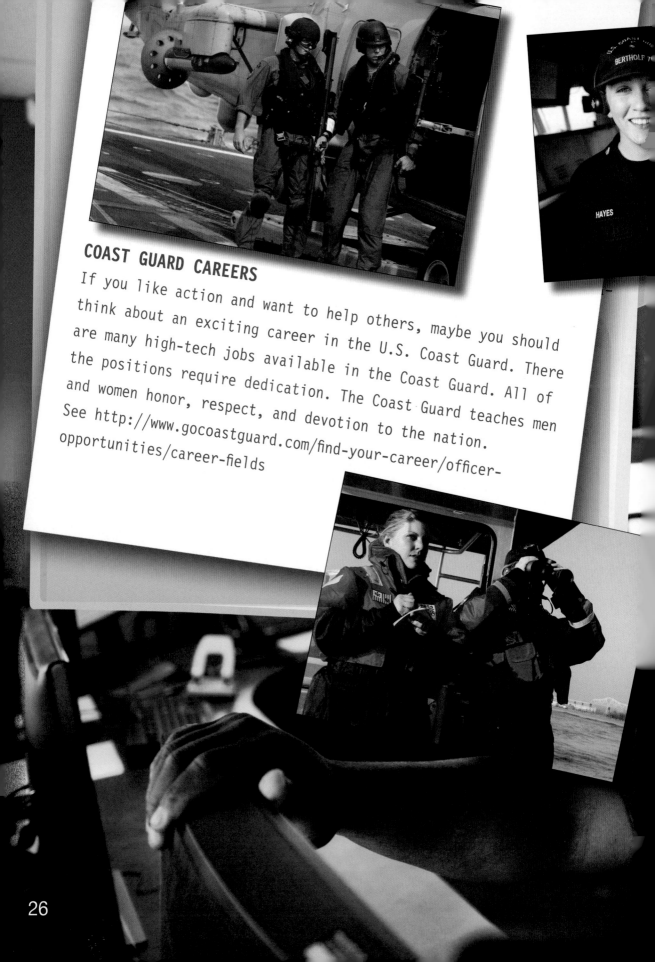

COAST GUARD CAREERS

If you like action and want to help others, maybe you should think about an exciting career in the U.S. Coast Guard. There are many high-tech jobs available in the Coast Guard. All of the positions require dedication. The Coast Guard teaches men and women honor, respect, and devotion to the nation. See http://www.gocoastguard.com/find-your-career/officer-opportunities/career-fields

TIMELINE

1790:
10 cutter vessels built, early beginnings of what is now the U.S. Coast Guard.

1861:
Received official name of Revenue Cutter Service.

1861-1864:
Acted as firing support and patrols during the American Civil War.

1915:
Officially renamed the U.S. Coast Guard.

1914-1918:
Cutters had convoy duties in European waters during World War I.

1917:
The Espionage Act gave the Coast Guard more power to protect merchant ships from sabotage

1980:
The Mariel Boatlife is the largest search and rescue operation since World War II.

1989:
Exxon Valdez oil spill in Alaska.

1990:
Port Security units are ordered to the Persian Gulf.

1879:
Bering Sea Patrol
initiated.

1897-1898:
Accomplished Point
Barrow-Overland Relief
Expedition.

1904:
Pioneered ship
to shore radio
communications.

1939:
Lighthouse
Service merged
with Coast Guard.

1939-1945:
Sank German U-boats.
Monitored and
captured Japanese
merchant vessels
during World War II.

1971:
Coast Guard has
more authority
over recreational
boating.

2001:
Terrorists attacks
on World Trade
Center. USCG are
some of the first
responders to help
victims.

2003:
Coast Guard deployed
to Southwest Asia as
part of Operation
Iraqi Freedom.

2010:
Deepwater Horizon
rig explosion and
oil spill.

UNITED STATES COAST GUARD

SEMPER PARATUS
1790

SHOW WHAT YOU KNOW

1. What year was the Coast Guard officially renamed?
2. Name three main duties of the Coast Guard.
3. Name equipment, other than ships that the Coast Guard uses.
4. What role does the Coast Guard play in helping sea life?
5. In what ways does the Coast Guard help victims of natural disasters?

GLOSSARY

contraband (KON-truh-band): goods brought illegally from one place to another

convoy (KON-voi): a group of military vehicles that travel together

cyber attacks (SYE-buhr uh-TAKSS): attacks carried out by using computer programs and the Internet

fleet (FLEET): a group of warships

foreign (FOR-uhn): coming from another country

humanitarian (hyoo-man-uh-TER-ee-uhn): to do with helping people and providing relief to those who are suffering

migrants (MYE-gruhntss): people who move from one country to another

offensive (uh-FEN-siv): a military attack

pollution (puh-LOO-shuhn): harmful materials that contaminate the earth, water, or air

smugglers (SMUHG-luhrz): people who bring products or drugs into a country illegally

trafficking (TRAF-ik-ing): transporting, trading or selling people or products across borders illegally

Index

Websites to Visit

http://www.uscg.mil/history/uscghist/Mascots.asp

http://www.seascout.org/

http://www.sdmaritime.org/the-ships/

About the Author

Piper Welsh is a writer who lives in Montana. She likes
to tour famous battleships and military forts across the
United States.

Meet The Author!
www.meetREMauthors.com